a morning cup of prayer for friends

CRANE HILL
PUBLISHERS

Scriptures taken from the HOLY BIBLE: NEW INTERNATIONAL VERSION®. NIV®. Copyright© 1973, 1978, 1984 by International Bible Society. Used by permission of The Zondervan Corporation.

"A Morning Cup of" is a registered trademark of Crane Hill Publishers, Inc.

Published by Crane Hill Publishers
www.cranehill.com

Book design by Miles G. Parsons
Illustrations by Tim Rocks and Christena Brooks
Cover art by Christena Brooks

Printed in China

Library of Congress Cataloging-in-Publication Data

Bright-Fey, J. (John)
   A morning cup of prayer for friends / John Bright-Fey. -- Crane Hill ed.
      p. cm.
   ISBN-13: 978-1-57587-263-6
   ISBN-10: 1-57587-263-3
   1. Prayer--Christianity. 2. Prayers. I. Title.
   BV210.3.B75 2006
   248.3'2--dc22

2006016160

a morning cup of prayer®

for friends

A daily guided devotional for a lifetime of inspiration and peace

john a. bright-fey

CRANE HILL
PUBLISHERS

Acknowledgments

I would like to thank the following individuals for their invaluable help and advice. This Morning Cup would surely not taste as sweet without their assistance:

To Professor Tom Gibbs for talking me into teaching college classes on prayer and contemplative living;
To all of my students whose experience of prayer and faith has profoundly moved me and deeply informed my work;
To Ellen, Linda, and all the staff and artists at Crane Hill Publishers for giving me this glorious opportunity;
To my amazing wife, Kim, who helps me in more ways than she could possibly know;
To the many men and women of faith that have, through the years, guided and shaped my life of prayer.

I thank God for each of you.

Dedication

In Loving Memory
Viola Gertrude Patricia Caverlee Marshall
"Grandma Vi"

Thanks for teaching me how to listen.

Contents

Foreword 9

Friendship and Prayer.................................... 11

Praying for the Needs of Others 17

What Is Prayer? 23

Why Should We Pray for Others? 33

Prayer: A Friend's Guide 37

Prayers for Friends 47

An Extra Sip: Prayerwalking......................... 59

A Friend's Prayer Journal 71

For I know the plans I have for you, declares the Lord, plans to prosper you and not to harm you, plans to give you hope and a future. Then you will call upon me and come and pray to me, and I will listen to you. You will seek me and find me when you seek me with all your heart.
—*Jeremiah* 29: 11-13

Foreword

Would you like your friends and acquaintances to have closer contact with God? If your answer is "Yes," then this book was written for you. With it, you can begin an incredible journey that will deeply influence the lives of those around you. The means to begin this journey and the power to sustain it are the same: prayer.

Part devotional and part instruction manual, this *Morning Cup of Prayer* is designed to be a spiritual patchwork quilt of advice, wisdom, and inspiration. With it you will learn to live a life of prayerful love and service for others.

I've tried to write this book so that you would be able to absorb its contents as easily as possible. As you give it your attention, consider it within the context of your own career, devotional path, and religious life.

I say that "I wrote" this book, but, in truth, my hand was guided by God and its contents formed by His Grace. I felt His love with every word. Now, it is my sincerest wish that you feel it as well and in the spirit of true friendship, pass it on to the rest of the world.

Friendship and Prayer

There are so many people in the world today that, simply, do not pray.

I first became aware of this years ago when a friend of mine came to me in great need. We talked for hours about his problem and looked at his situation from every possible angle. When it became clear that we were going over old ground, I suggested that we pray for guidance. "Pray?" he said to me, "John, it's been so long, I wouldn't know where to start."

This is a thoroughly sad situation because so many of today's problems yield readily to prayer's power. Prayer can change the course of an individual life or the life of a nation. It can help us solve the most perplexing of problems. Families torn apart by strife, disaster, or indifference can be made whole again with prayer. It can cure the worst physical illnesses and heal the deepest emotional wounds. If we become lost, it helps us to find our way again.

Prayer knows. It pulls us back from the brink of what is toxic and shows us where and when to move forward towards nourishment. Most importantly, prayer is our birthright as God's children. It energizes, strengthens, comforts, informs, supports and protects us. Simply put, prayer reclaims lives, futures, and souls.

With all that prayer has to offer, why then don't more people pray? The answer is simple: they don't know how.

Perhaps you know people who need the complete wholeness that prayer provides but are so embroiled in their own turmoil and suffering they don't feel able to pray themselves. Maybe they have never prayed before or have been turned off by prayer for one reason or another.

Do you have an out-of-state friend that needs the gift of prayer? How often do you see a complete stranger who is desperately in need of the blessings and power of prayer? What do you do? You know that praying for these people is important but how do you go about it? Maybe—just maybe—you would like to lead a prayerful life that's deep enough to allow you to regularly pray for others in need.

If you would like to be a friend in prayer but don't quite know how, when, or where to go about it, the book you are holding will answer those questions. It will help clear the path and show you the way to be a true and loving friend through God's gift of prayer.

I've divided this book into roughly three parts. The first will be a discussion of the special needs of friends that can be addressed by prayer. No matter what the nature or source of the problem or who is having it, the key to its resolution can be found in His promise of prayer.

The second part of this book will be a discussion of the mechanics of prayer and some of its methods. I will also discuss what a prayerful life can look like.

Most often, when someone tells me, "I don't pray," what they are really saying is, "I don't know what to say to God." If you are one of those individuals, please don't worry. In the third part of this book, I will present you with an assortment of Biblically based prayers and relevant passages from His Word that both support and augment them.

Each scriptural prayer was written especially to meet the needs of those who actively participate in His Holy Work by praying for the needs of others. They are grouped with the scripture passages that I've found most helpful for contemplation and prayer in this regard. Take your time with each of them and, I believe, you will find much wisdom.

Please look upon these prayers as suggestions. True prayer is a profoundly personal thing that must come from your heart. Think of the prayers and passages in this book as starting points for your personal spiritual journey as a friend in prayer. Use them to get comfortable with the act of praying for others. Then, as guided by the Holy Spirit, you will learn to speak the language of prayer.

In the time it would take for you to have a pleasant cup of tea, you can begin your spiritual journey as a friend in prayer and sustain the practice for a lifetime. More importantly, you can help bring the blessings and grace of our Father to those in need. Soon, you will sit in the Spirit with dear friends both near and far while sharing a cup of God's love. But before then, would you like to share a Morning Cup with me?

JBF
Birmingham, Alabama
2006

What a Friend we have in Jesus, all our sins and griefs to bear!
What a privilege to carry everything to God in prayer!
O what peace we often forfeit, O what needless pain we bear,
All because we do not carry everything to God in prayer.

Have we trials and temptations? Is there trouble anywhere?
We should never be discouraged; take it to the Lord in prayer.
Can we find a friend so faithful who will all our sorrows share?
Jesus knows our every weakness; take it to the Lord in prayer.

Are we weak and heavy laden, cumbered with a load of care?
Precious Savior, still our refuge, take it to the Lord in prayer.
Do your friends despise, forsake you? Take it to the Lord in prayer!
In His arms He'll take and shield you; you will find a solace there.

Blessed Savior, Thou hast promised Thou wilt all our burdens bear
May we ever, Lord, be bringing all to Thee in earnest prayer.
Soon in glory bright unclouded there will be no need for prayer
Rapture, praise and endless worship will be our sweet portion there.

Joseph Scriven

Praying for the Needs of Others

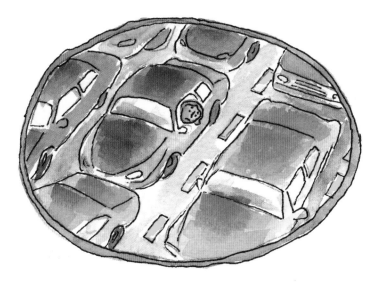

My grandmother, a gifted music teacher, was the first person to make me aware of Joseph Scriven and his wonderful poem. Scriven, born in Ireland in 1819, was a man who took his faith seriously. Living in Port Hope, Ontario, he could regularly be found performing all sorts of work and menial tasks for those less fortunate than himself.

Frequently, Scriven would carry a sawhorse with him as he walked through the town of Port Hope and cut wood for those who didn't have the money to pay for firewood themselves. He worked for the sick and the infirm, all the while refusing to accept wages or compensation of any kind. Even in the face of personal tragedy, Joseph Mendicott Scriven continued working to ease the pain of others. The people of Port Hope felt blessed by the presence of this kind man, who was a friend to all.

In his late thirties, Scriven fell very ill. One of his friends who came to comfort him during the sickness, discovered a poem by Scriven titled, "Pray Without Ceasing." Scriven had written it for his own mother in Dublin to ease her suffering during a long illness. He claimed that he and God had written it together expressly for his mother and it didn't seem right to publish it as his own. That having been said, it was published and eventually set to music by Charles Converse in 1868. Converse entitled his piece "What A Friend We Have In Jesus" and since then, it has been one of our most beloved and beautiful hymns.

And pray in the Spirit on all occasions with all kinds of prayers and requests. With this in mind, be alert and always keep on praying for all the saints.
—*Ephesians 6:18*

The poem/hymn of Joseph Scriven tells us that our greatest friend is Jesus Christ. The story of his life tells us that there are always people who need our help and, no matter where we are or what our own situation, we can come to their aid.

"What A Friend We Have In Jesus" can serve as a perfect model for identifying those that need our prayers. Those in pain or grief, those who are suffering great temptation, and those troubled and in turmoil can all use our prayers. Who might some of those people be?

- Friends and acquaintances
- Family members
- Victims of natural disasters
- Victims of crime and violence
- Our teachers
- Our nation's military
- Our troops in harm's way
- The president and all governmental leaders
- The nations of the world
- The people involved in current events anywhere in the world

You can pray for literally anyone in the world who you think needs the grace of our heavenly Father. You can even treat situations and circumstances as if they are people and pray for them as well. After all, aren't situations and circumstances ultimately made up of individuals? Regarding the subject of praying for others, you are only as limited as your imagination. But here is the most important thing; in your heart, you must see them as friends.

Jesus was sent to save us all, even those who turn away from Him. I believe that, when guided by the Holy Spirit, each of us knows full well the extent of our gifts and our deficits. We intrinsically know what to do to conquer our fears and address those issues that stand between us and our being the person God knows us to be. We have but to do it. Sometimes the prayers of others are all that we need to go that extra mile, to be healed physically, emotionally, or spiritually.

We all need help at one time or another. We all need firewood when we can least afford it. And while we have the greatest friend in Jesus Christ, couldn't we also use the prayerful friendship of our brothers and sisters? Couldn't they use ours? I think you know the answer:

"Are we weak and heavy laden, cumbered with a load of care? Precious Savior, still our refuge, take it to the Lord in prayer."

What Is Prayer?

The stated goal of this book is to teach you to pray for other people—to be a true friend in God. In order to do that, we need a definition of precisely what "praying" is. We also need to discuss the different kinds of prayer and the best ways to approach them. Before we get much further, though, I have a story that might help us get things off to a good start and insure a great finish.

An Example of Prayer

My inspiration for this book on prayer and the model I use for conducting a prayerful life come from a woman very near and dear to me. Time and again, she showed me the power or prayer, love, and the wonders of true friendship.

Everything I know about prayer I learned from my maternal grandmother, Viola. Grandma Vi was a devout churchgoer and easily the most amazing Christian that you'd ever be likely to meet. To be fair, I've learned a lot about prayer, contemplation, and devotion from many other wonderful men and women of faith. But the lessons from Grandma remain to this day the most profound, direct, and the most useful that I've ever received. Everything she did—whether it was homemaking, teaching music, comforting a friend or being a wife and grandmother—she approached with prayer.

Every morning after putting away the breakfast dishes, Grandma Vi would quietly announce that she was going to her room to "talk with God." She would then retire to the back bedroom, close the door, and do precisely that. Forty-five minutes to an hour later, she would emerge renewed, refreshed—transformed really—confident, self assured and positively radiant.

No matter what difficulties life presented her, the negative would literally fade away as her smile and countenance pushed back the gloom. The grace she radiated was as palpable and real as gravity. You could feel it; you could almost hold it in your hand. No matter what kind of ugly mood had you by the scruff of the neck, her smile set you free. Grandma had just finished talking with God and everything was, profoundly, right with the world.

Talking with God

I cannot remember how young I was when I first realized that Grandma said, "talk with God" instead of the usual "talk to God" that most people say when discussing prayer. Indeed, the transformation that would occur within her bespoke of something much more than simply a one-sided long distance conversation. I mean, it looked like she and God had actually been sitting in her room having a chat!

When I asked her what she and God talked about, she would reply, "Oh, all kinds of things." "Big stuff?" I asked. "Yes," she said "but, small things, too. I ask Him to watch over you and the rest of the family. If I have a problem I ask for His help and the strength to take care of it the way that He wants me to. I thank Him for all of the happiness and blessings He has given me. Most of the time, though, God talks and I listen to Him. You have to listen if you're going to have a real conversation with God. He likes it when we listen, just the way I like it when you listen to me. After all, He loves me the way that I love you."

"Do you only talk to God in your room?" I asked. "No," she said. " He meets me here." As she spoke she touched my heart with her hand. "I talk with Him here." That made me feel good and I remember thinking in a child's way that while it was important to love God, it was far more important to let Him love you.

In the same way, the Spirit helps us in our weakness. We do not know what we ought to pray for, but the Spirit himself intercedes for us with groans that words cannot express..
—Romans 8:26

Any Time, Any Place, Any Thing, Any Subject

As I grew older, my fascination with prayer grew, as did my love for God. Yes, our relationship had its rocky moments, but pop culture and arrogant churchmen aside, I never lost contact with Him or forgot how important it was to surrender to His Grace.

Grandma Vi continued to amaze me with her gifts of prayer. When I would drive the twelve hours from college to my grandparents' trailer in Bossier City, Louisiana, she would, quite literally, pray me in. Think about it; she would go about her daily chores with half of her attention actively engaged in a twelve-hour-long continuous prayer for my safe journey. Frequently, she'd have a "message from God" for me when I arrived at the trailer, along with a warm embrace and a home cooked meal that was fit for, well, Jehovah.

Later, when I was rested and ready to drive the additional three hours to home, she would smile and say, "Be careful and be sure to call me when you get to your Mom's house so I know when to quit praying." No matter what time it was, she wouldn't go to sleep until she'd received my call.

I have no doubt that even after I called the trailer to let her know of my safe arrival, she continued to pray. It was clear to me that her whole life was a prayer. That was what I wanted for myself and, over the years, it became what I wanted for everyone else.

Grandma made it plain; a person could—and should—have a heartfelt conversation with God anytime, anywhere, under any circumstances, and about anything.

Different Kinds of Prayer

Grandma's prayers on my behalf were an example of Intercessory prayer, where one person prays for another. There are other kinds of prayer as well.

There are prayers of Thanksgiving and of Praise where we thank our Heavenly Father for the blessings He has given us and give honor to His Grace and Perfect Will. We can obtain more of God through Seeking prayer wherein we simply announce our intention to rest in His presence and allow Him to speak through His Word. Prayers of Confession allow you to repent your sins and ask your Father for the blessing of His forgiveness. Prayers of Supplication involve asking God for His Divine intervention. Submissive prayer or prayers of Surrender involve completely opening up to Gods love and welcoming His Grace and Will into our lives.

Different Ways to Pray

Just as there are different kinds of prayer, there are also different ways to pray. You may talk with God silently or aloud. You may mindfully and deliberately repeat passages from the Bible while pondering the meaning of His Word. This is called Repetitive prayer. Prayer can be performed Reflectively by sitting still and coming to know God through the peace of silence or by reflecting on the deeper meaning of His hand at work in your life.

The Most Important Thing about Prayer

Don't let the different kinds of prayer or the different ways to pray confuse you. Remember Grandma Vi's model:

You talk with God (that means listening as well as talking)

- Anytime,
- Anywhere,
- (under) Any circumstances,
- (about) Anything.
- ?

But something is missing. What's vitally important is that your prayers be authentic, that is, they must come from your heart and be in your own voice. Even if you are reading a Biblically based prayer composed by someone else, you must make it real for you. You must see it, feel it, taste it, and touch it with everything you've got. So now we have our final "A": Authentically.

You Talk With God

- Anytime
- Anywhere
- Any Circumstances
- Anything
- Authentically

*So do not fear, for I am with you; do not be dismayed,
for I am your God. I will strengthen you and help you;
I will uphold you with my righteous right hand.*
—Isaiah 4:10

*He has showed you, O man, what is good. And what
does the Lord require of you? To act justly and to love
mercy and to walk humbly with your God.*
—Micah 6:8

*Surely goodness and love will follow me all the days of
my life, and I will dwell in the house of the Lord forever.*
—Psalm 23:6

Why Should We Pray for Others?

There are so many good reasons for you to pray for other people. To start with, reread the list on page 19. All of those problems and circumstances can be addressed and solved with prayer. But there are other reasons as well. You can pray:

- for spiritual growth
- for material needs
- for protection from evil
- to confess your sins and ask for forgiveness
- for the sins of others
- for the needs of others
- for the church and its missions
- for others to receive His Word

- for personal healing
- for others to be healed
- for wisdom about any subject
- to help simplify your life
- for personal direction
- to participate in His holy work around the world

The list could go on forever. When it comes to prayer, you are only as limited as your imagination.

I tell you the truth, my Father will give you whatever you ask in my name. Until now you have not asked for anything in my name. Ask and you will receive, and your joy will be complete.
—John 16:23-24

Prayer is a wonderful gift from our Heavenly Father. He places great value on it and we should avail ourselves of it. So much can be accomplished through the power of prayer. You have but to read the stories of Moses, Samson, Elijah, and the apostle Peter in the Bible to grasp its potential.*

Yet, so often, we feel like we don't have the time or the energy for prayer. Many of us lead such busy lives. Our minds and our bodies work overtime to accomplish the many things we must in order to fulfill our earthly obligations. But when we stop to pray, even if only for a few moments, our whole being changes. We slow our frantic pace, focus on God, and say, "Lord, I love you with all my heart and soul."

Whenever anyone asks me why they should pray for others, I remind them that everyone needs our love. It is our Christian duty to help. Prayer allows us to participate in God's work around the world. Whenever anyone asks me why they should pray at all, rather than listing the reasons I say this: "Your Heavenly Father loves you dearly and wants you to visit with Him often. He wants you to come to Him for rest, advice, encouragement, and all manner of council. You can visit anytime you want, day or night. Calling ahead isn't necessary because He is always home waiting for you, His beloved child. There amid the beats of His heart, you will surely find nourishment, comfort, and joy. You will find meaning and direction. If you come to Him when you are sick, He will heal you. No matter how many people are cruel to you or how much life has beaten you down, you can always go to your Father's home. You can tell Him anything and He will be there for you. All you have to do is show up. The doorway to His heart is His son Jesus Christ and the key to that doorway is prayer." Now that sounds like reason enough for me. How about you?

*Moses (Exodus 15:24-26); Samson (Judges 16:28-30); Elijah (James 5:17,18); Peter (Acts 9:36-41).

I urge, then, first of all, that requests, prayers, intercession and thanksgiving be made for everyone—for kings and all those in authority, that we may live peaceful and quiet lives in all godliness and holiness. This is good, and pleases God our Savior, who wants all men to be saved and to come to a knowledge of the truth.
—1 Timothy 2:1-4

Be joyful always; pray continually; give thanks in all circumstances, for this is God's will for you in Jesus Christ.
—1 Thessalonians 5:16-18

Prayer: A Friend's Guide

*But when you pray, go into your room, close the door
and pray to your Father, who is unseen. Then your
Father, who sees what is done in secret, will reward you.*
—Matthew 6:6

 ## Step One:
Set the Stage with Solitude, Silence, and Stillness

Do you remember how Grandma Vi would go into her room to pray? She was following the instructions laid out in Matthew 6:6. It's the very first thing you should do before you pray: find a place of solitude and enter it.

Your place of solitude can be a room or the corner of a room. It can be your back porch. In truth, it doesn't even have to be a physical structure. Your place of solitude can be out of doors in the deep woods or a even a public park filled with people. It can be any place where you can engineer a feeling of being alone.

When you enter into solitude you enter into the realm of the soul. Here, God gives you the opportunity to drop all pretense and simply be yourself. When you are in solitude you are never really alone. You and your Heavenly Father are there together. That is His promise.

After entering into the realm of the soul, you should then embrace silence and stillness. Here's how you do it.

Generally relax, accept the guidance of the Holy Spirit and tell yourself that you are preparing for prayer, preparing to talk with God. Close your eyes and briefly watch your body and how it naturally moves. For example, your chest rises and falls as you breathe. That's okay; just let it. Perhaps you notice some tension in your neck so you gently drop your shoulders downward a bit to release it. If you notice any physical movement at all, just take notice of it and say to yourself that you'd like to sit as still as you are comfortably able.

Turn your attention to your mind. Other than focusing on God and your intention to pray, don't try to control it in any way. Try not to chastise yourself for a wandering mind that jumps around in the background from one mental topic to the next. Simply acknowledge that your mind is doing something, casually watch it unfold, and keep your focus on your Father and His presence.

You may find it helpful, as opportunity allows, to have soothing music accompany your preparations for prayer. If so, you will enjoy the Morning Cup Audio CD that accompanies this volume. It was designed especially to set the tone for your prayer time.

Settling into a time of prayer is like watching a river flow by out of the corner of your eye. You'll notice obvious things like sailboats, motor craft, tree limbs floating on the surface, even the occasional duck. There are birds flying above the river and fish you cannot see swimming beneath its surface. You're sitting in one place with God but all of the life that is the river flows past you. Enjoy yourself. After all, you are preparing to talk with God. What could be better than that?

Put a light smile on your face as you allow the river of your mind to float by and you'll begin to notice something: your mind will settle down, your body will relax, and you will begin to feel quiet all over. Sometimes it feels as if you are sensing all of your parts all at once. The best word I know of to describe your sensation is "quiescence." Every part of you settles down and you will feel organized and peaceful. You become bathed in God's Grace and Presence. Now you are ready. This is the canvas upon which you will present your prayers.

It Only Takes a Moment

Though you could spend a lot of time completing your preparations for prayer, it really only takes a moment to engineer solitude, silence, and stillness. With practice you'll be able to set the stage for prayer in an instant.

There is benefit in setting the stage and resting in the realm of the soul for longer periods of time. In this way you utilize solitude, silence, and stillness to reflect and listen for God's wisdom and guidance. There in His loving embrace, you will experience genuine tranquility and perfect peace of mind.

Step Two:
Embrace a Prayerful Attitude

Prayer is so very much more than mere words. It is an attitude that reflects our most heartfelt wishes and hopes. In reality, it's all about heart—your heart to God's heart.

We are all God's children. As a parent He isn't gruff or unfeeling, yet we often approach Him as if He is. Our Father is love itself and the secret to true prayer is simple: we must be His children.

I often ask people who pray regularly to listen to themselves as they pray. "Try it for yourself," I say. "How do you sound when you pray? Do you sound like an outsider intruding upon God's quiet repose? Do you plead or beg? Do your words impose or do you sound like a child talking with a beloved parent?"

That last example, of course, is how it should be. We should not sound like spiritual panhandlers. We are God's loving and obedient children and behaving in that way is the secret key to true and authentic prayer.

Unique Friends Are
Heartfelt Friends

In His wisdom, our Heavenly Father created each of us to be a unique individual. When He gave us the gift of prayer He knew that each of us would have our own unique way of speaking with Him. That's precisely the way He wants it. He wants each of us to be completely honest and authentic by expressing what's in our heart to Him. Remember, whether you offer spontaneous prayers or prayers composed by someone else, you must feel it in your heart.

Step Three:
Choose Your Method of Prayer

There are many ways that you can pray for your friends. For this Morning Cup I've chosen four ways that you may engage in prayer:

Spoken Prayer

Simply put, speak aloud. Declaiming your prayers out loud has a special quality to it. When you taste what you are saying, the words have a greater effect upon you and your prayers become powerful.

Silent Prayer

Silent prayers are more intimate than spoken ones. Praying in this way brings a delicate and private quality to your worship. Use silent prayer whenever you feel the need to more personally connect with your Heavenly Father.

Repetitive Prayer

Repeat your prayer over and over. You may do this aloud or silently in your mind. However, no matter how you choose to say the prayer, it is important that each repetition be mindful and deliberate. Mindlessly repeating words is not praying. Repetitive, authentic prayer produces a profoundly focused communication with God.

Reflective Prayer

Reflective prayer is performed in silence. Simply read a Biblical passage or any prayer that you choose and silently reflect on its meaning. Just hold the thought of the prayer in your heart and mind. The Holy Spirit does the rest. Reflective prayer engenders peaceful communication with God and reveals His Wisdom.

♥ Step Four: ♥
Talk with God

All of the prayers that make up the balance of this book have been composed, and the Bible selections chosen, with the idea of using them in any one of the above prayer methods outlined in Step Three. Of course, you can dispense with them altogether and speak with your Father according to the dictates of your heart. But what if you have never prayed before?

Do you remember my comments in the beginning about people who say that they don't know how to pray for other people? All too often, they really just don't know what to say to God. If you are one of those people then you probably remember that I also told you not to worry.

The next section of this book contains all the suggestions you need to learn how to speak the language of prayer. Please learn from it and let it inspire you to lead a prayerful life. Your Father is in His home and He would dearly love to speak with you.

Step Five:
Listen to God

The fifth and final step of prayer is probably the most important. At least it was for Grandma Vi. Do you remember what she said about how she spent most of her prayer time? That's right; she spent it listening.

Please remember, authentic prayer is a conversation filled with devotion and love that takes place between you and your Heavenly Father. Prayer is so incredibly precious to God. It releases an enormous outpouring of His wisdom, power, inspiration, and strength. But you have to listen and you have to listen patiently.

After speaking to Him, ask God to speak back to you in any way He sees fit. You may use the journal that begins on page 71 to record any important thoughts and insights that come up, especially when He speaks to you through His Word. Let Him call your attention to those areas in your life where He wants to help.

Spend as much time listening to God as you would like. One minute of really listening to God would be great. Fifteen would be so much better. You choose. An hour listening to God isn't too much, and neither is a lifetime.

Let us then labor for an inward stillness,
An inward stillness and an inward healing;
That perfect silence where lips and heart
Are still, and we no longer entertain
Our own imperfect thoughts and vain opinions,
But God alone speaks in us, and we wait
In singleness of heart, that we may know
God's will, and in the silence of our spirit,
That we may do God's will and do that only.
—Longfellow, The Christus

A Life of Friendship Inspired by Prayer

I've always loved the word "inspired." It means, "in-spirit." When my publisher approached me to write several books on prayer for the Morning Cup series she could hardly have known that on those mornings after my grandmother had chatted with God, she would, invariably, make a cup of tea, sit down, leisurely sip, and bask in the glow of being "in spirit." I can think of no better way to start a day or spend a life. Can you?

The Lord's Prayer

This, then, is how you should pray:
 "Our Father in heaven,
 hallowed be your name,

your kingdom come,
 your will be done
 on earth as it is in heaven.

Give us today our daily bread.
Forgive us our debts,
 as we also have forgiven our debtors.

And lead us not into temptation,
 but deliver us from the evil one."
—*Matthew 6:9-13*

Prayers for Friends

Whenever you see a friend mired in the trials of life, it is time to surrender through prayer. And even though they may be too confused, nervous, or uncertain to pray for themselves, you can show your love by praying for them. Authentic prayer is a fundamental rededication of your faith every time you engage in it. It brings the peace of the Father to you by helping you to completely open up to His love, wisdom, strength, and forgiveness.

Relax your heart and bring peace to your soul by surrendering all of your cares and worries to God through prayer. What doubts could you possibly have when you are resting in your Father's loving arms while being filled with His Grace?

Prayers

As you begin to incorporate prayer into your life, you may find it helpful to have examples of prayers to get you started. Here are some samples that, along with selected scripture passages, will set the tone for prayer. As you make these initial steps, the Holy Spirit will help you in your efforts.

A Prayer of Dedication

Father, in the name of Jesus, I surrender to the Holy Spirit. Fill my soul with Your Grace and let me lead the life that You have set out for me. Let me of service to others and spread Your Word through my deeds. Amen.

*That if you confess with your mouth, "Jesus is Lord,"
and believe in your heart that God raised him from the
dead, you will be saved. For it is with your heart that
you believe and are justified, and it is with your mouth
that you confess and are saved.*
—Romans 10:9-10

A Prayer of Acceptance

Father, I accept Your grace with humility and gratitude. Thank You for being my guide and companion. In You I find peace and am able to rest on my journey. Amen.

I am still confident of this:
I will see the goodness of the LORD
in the land of the living.
Wait for the LORD;
be strong and take heart
and wait for the LORD.
—*Psalm* 27:13-14

A Prayer of Devotion

Heavenly Father, I offer myself to You as a
sacrifice of flesh, blood, and bone; a living
sacrifice whose only goals are to be Your devoted
child and to do Your Will. Amen.

*Therefore, I urge you, brothers, in view of God's mercy,
to offer your bodies as living sacrifices, holy and
pleasing to God—this is your spiritual act of worship.
—Romans 12:1*

A Prayer for Help in Time of Need

Dearest Father, I am very sad. I stand before You in the hope that You will grant me Your Grace in this time of need. I am discouraged because all of my efforts seem futile. Here and now, I will open my heart and put all of my faith and trust in You. In You I will find peace and I will be redeemed. Amen.

Listen to my prayer, O God,
do not ignore my plea;
hear me and answer me.
My thoughts trouble me and I am distraught
—Psalm 55:1-2

Fear of man will prove to be a snare,
but whoever trusts in the LORD is kept safe.
—*Proverbs 29:25*

A Prayer for Comfort

Lord, I come before You to ask for Your aid and
mercy in my time of need. Father, because of all
the suffering I see in the world, I have given
myself over to fear. Even though I know the fear
to be false, it has caused me to be hesitant and to
misstep. I find myself withdrawing from others
and ignoring their needs. I am heartedly sorry for
behaving in this way. In the name of Christ Jesus,
I reaffirm my commitment to be unafraid and to
do good for everyone who needs it. Amen.

Therefore, as we have opportunity, let us do good to all people, especially to those who belong to the family of believers.
—Galatians 6:10

The entire law is summed up in a single command: "Love your neighbor as yourself."
—Galatians 5:14

A friend loves at all times, and a brother is born for adversity.
—Proverbs 17:17

A Prayer for Strength

Heavenly Father, I know that I am Your child and that You have made me strong and courageous. Help me to honor my strength, which flows from You. I know that the wickedness of the world which intimidates me only appears real. You are the One reality in which all should take refuge. With You by my side I will stay the course and act firmly and resolutely in accord with Your wishes. I will watch over my friends and pray for the sins of the world. In Jesus' name I pray, Amen.

A Prayer for Serving Others

Heavenly Father, I know that You sent Your only Son to save us so that we might fully participate in Your Holy work. I pledge to use my talents to serve the needs of my brothers and sisters in Christ. Amen.

... who has saved us and called us to a holy life—not
because of anything we have done but because of His
own purpose and grace. This grace was given us in
Christ Jesus before the beginning of time ...
—2 Timothy 1:9

A Prayer for Discernment

Lord, help me to show the world Your Way. I
pray that everyone may share the gifts of the
world according to your Divine plan. Please show
me those in physical, mental, and spiritual need
and watch over me as I help them in Jesus' name.
Amen.

Brothers, if someone is caught in a sin, you who are spiritual should restore him gently. But watch yourself, or you also may be tempted. Carry each other's burdens, and in this way you will fulfill the law of Christ.
—Galatians 6:1-2

Live in harmony with one another. Do not be proud, but be willing to associate with people of low position. Do not be conceited.
—Romans 12:16

A Prayer for Wisdom

Father, grant me Your wisdom so that I may help my fellow man to turn away from evil and embrace righteousness. Amen.

*Even though I am not physically present, I am with
you in spirit. And I have already passed judgment on
the one who did this, just as if I were present. When
you are assembled in the name of our Lord Jesus and I
am with you in spirit, and the power of our Lord Jesus
is present, hand this man over to Satan, so that the
sinful nature may be destroyed and his spirit saved on
the day of the Lord.*
—1 Corinthians 5:3-5

An Extra Sip

Prayerwalking

Whenever you feel the pace of life start to run over you, it's time for walking prayers or Prayerwalking.

Every time you take a step you have the opportunity for prayer. In many ways, walking prayers can have more impact on you than standing, kneeling, or sitting while you pray. This is because your entire body is in motion when you walk just as it is when you are going about your daily tasks. It is instrumental in teaching you how to pray during any activity and, eventually, to pray without ceasing.

Prayerwalking intrinsically reminds us of our connection to God's miracle, that is the earth. When we walk we feel it beneath our feet. We know it with our whole body just as we know about our Heavenly connection to our Father through our souls. Walking prayers enliven your senses, clear your thinking, and can energize you to God's Word. If you ever need reaffirmation of your chosen path in life or if you are having a hard time standing your ground for what you believe in, then pray as you walk.

Walking prayers are best done when you are alone. Anywhere you can walk slowly and deliberately will be suitable for these prayers. I prefer the outdoors, be it a city park, the woods, or your backyard. The choice is yours. It is important to bring a sense of stillness to your walk.

Pretend that the prayers are delicate and that a hurried pace might break them. Be gentle with yourself. As you walk among the many gifts that He has placed for us in this world, know that each step you take brings you closer to Him.

If you choose to walk in a public place, be sure not to call attention to what you are doing. But take the opportunity to pray for people you see along the way. If you pass someone who is obviously ill, then pray for them. If you see someone giving into sin, pray for their deliverance. You can walk around your home, garden, campus, or city hall and bring the power of prayer with you everywhere. Simply, walk and talk with God.

Walking Prayers

I walk with God in peace and contentment.
I walk with God and recognize His gifts to
me.
I walk with God and am nourished by His
loving kindness.
I walk with God and am healed and
strengthened by His Grace.
I walk with God and extend His love to
everyone.
I walk with God knowing that He is with me
always.
I walk with God and am filled with the Holy
Spirit.
I walk with God and breathe in His mercy.
I walk with God knowing His Perfect Will.
I walk with God upon a bedrock of His Word
and bring the light of His message to the
world.
In Jesus' name I pray, Amen.

A Prayer for Guidance

Lord, show me the road that leads to You.

A new command I give you: Love one another. As I have loved you, so you must love one another.
—John 13:34

A Prayer for Love

Father, help me to sow the seeds of Your love everywhere I walk. In Jesus' name, I will cultivate the world and plant Your seeds of love in every heart I meet.

A Prayer for Forgiveness

Heavenly Father, let me forgive with each step
I take.

Lord, I walk in the comfort of Your forgiveness.
Please forgive those that have wronged me. No
matter what their transgression, Your forgiveness
will free them to love You as I do.

A Prayer for Grace

Lord, for all of my days I will walk in Your Grace.

A Prayer for Peace

Father, help me to realize the peace and
contentment of Your loving kindness. I will move
through my life without hurry and without worry.
Help me to experience everyone I meet as one
of Your children. Amen.

A Prayer for Deliverance

Heavenly Father, You sent Your loving Son Jesus
to walk among us so that we might see Your
truth and the truth of Your Word. In Jesus' name
I walk away from wickedness and evil. Amen.

A Prayer for Holiness

Lord, in Jesus' name I bless others and sanctify myself with every step. Even while involved in the most mundane of tasks, I know that each step shapes me for Your work. Please Lord, direct my feet so they carry me closer to You.

An Affirmation

Father, with each step I take I move deeply into myself as the Temple of the Holy Spirit. In Jesus' name, Amen.

I tell you the truth, whatever you bind on earth will be bound in heaven, and whatever you loose on earth will be loosed in heaven. Again, I tell you that if two of you on earth agree about anything you ask for, it will be done for you by my Father in heaven. For where two or three come together in my name, there I am with them.
—Matthew 18:18-20

A Friend's Prayer Journal

Have you ever wondered whether there is more spiritual life than you are currently experiencing? For most, the answer is usually, "Yes." It is perfectly fine and, I think, natural to expect something deeper, richer, and more profound from your spiritual life and a more complete experience of prayer is the key to realizing it. Use these pages to keep a journal about your new life of prayer. Write down whom or what you are praying for and use it as both a reminder and a way to stay on a prayerful track.

_____

_____

_____

_____

_____

_____

_____

_____

_____

_____

_____

_____

"When you pray, rather let your heart be
without words than your words without heart."
John Bunyan

_____

_____

_____

_____

_____

_____

_____

_____

_____

_____

_____

_____

"When you pray for anyone you tend to modify your personal attitude toward him."
Norman Vincent Peale

_____

_____

_____

_____

_____

_____

_____

_____

_____

_____

_____

"Rich is the person who has a praying friend."
Janice Hugh

"There is nothing that makes us love a man so much as praying for him."

William Law

About the Author

John Bright-Fey teaches classes on prayer, contemplation, and leading a prayerful life. He is the author of several books in the Morning Cup and Whole Heart series. He lives in Birmingham, Alabama.

You may also enjoy these other devotionals in the Morning Cup series. Each one would be a welcomed and treasured gift for the special people in your life.

A Morning Cup of® Prayer for Teachers

ISBN-13: 978-1-57587-265-0
ISBN-10: 1-57587-265-X

A Morning Cup of® Prayer for Mothers

ISBN-13: 978-1-57587-264-3
ISBN-10: 1-57587-264-1

A Morning Cup of® Prayer for Women

ISBN-13: 978-1-57587-266-7
ISBN-10: 1-57587-266-8

Prayer at a Glance

Prayer is talking with God

- Anytime
- Anywhere
- Under any circumstance
- About anything
- Authentically

 Step One: Set the stage with solitude, silence, and stillness.

 Step Two: Embrace a prayerful attitude.

 Step Three: Choose your method of prayer.

Step Four: Talk with God.

 Step Five: Listen to God.

Tear this page out and post it in a handy spot for quick reference to help you make time to pray.